LITTLE GREEN FIRETRUCK

Written by
William (BJ) Jetter

Illustrated by
Rob Penny

AuthorHouse™ UK Ltd.
500 Avebury Boulevard
Central Milton Keynes, MK9 2BE
www.authorhouse.co.uk
Phone: 08001974150

First published by AuthorHouse 4/3/2008

ISBN: 978-1-4343-5144-9 (sc)

Printed in the United States of America
Bloomington, Indiana

This book is printed on acid-free paper.

authorHOUSE®

This book is dedicated to my two grandsons:

Zachary & Parker

&

Rob's grandson:

Ethan

There once was a town called Berg. It was a small town where people from all parts of life lived. Berg was a growing little town with a bright future. In the center of town stood a single-story building with a huge garage door. On the front of the building was the name Berg Volunteer Fire Department. The biggest secret in the town of Berg rested behind the huge door of this building. The town of Berg had many types of buildings: a large school for the children of the town, a drug store, a shopping center, and a hardware store. Berg had many churches and a large park where the children of Berg played baseball, soccer, basketball, tennis, and football. For the small children, the park had a huge playground with a big sign that said "Children Only."

On special holidays, the town always celebrated with a big parade led by the biggest secret in town, Old Betsy. She was a grand old fire truck who was one of the bravest fire trucks ever made. Betsy's big red fenders and long pumper proved over the years to be one of the areas biggest secrets. You see Betsy's job was not only to lead the parades, but also to protect the town of Berg 24 hours a day, 365 days a year for over 50 years. Old Betsy kept a watchful eye over the town of Berg; she was always ready at a moment's notice to answer the call for help.

The town of Berg had a fire chief named Lou and a chief engineer named Ed. Both of these men, along with the other twenty-five men and women of the Berg Volunteer Fire Department, always knew Old Betsy was there to help them fight fires of all types and respond with her ladders to save cats in trees, pump water out of basements during heavy rains, and—most of all—help sick people.

Every Tuesday night, the twenty-five men and women would get together to practice their firefighting and rescue skills. Chief Lou would always say to his firefighters, "You have to know your equipment and know how to use it, but most of all you have to take good care of Old Betsy."

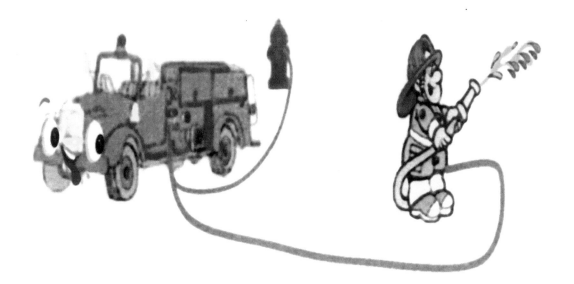

It was a Tuesday night in September, and the training was to test the hose in the firehouse and the hose stored on Old Betsy. Chief Engineer Ed hooked Betsy up to the fire hydrant and whispered to her, saying, "Betsy, how are you doing? You know we are going to put you through the paces tonight. We are going to work your pump to it fullest. Are you up to it?" Betsy smiled with a glimmer in her headlights and said, "Ed, let's give the new firefighters a workout, okay?" Ed said, "Betsy, you're the boss. Just let me know when it's time to stop working your pump and engine so hard." Betsy said, "Okay, Ed." After all the hoses were hooked up to all the pump outlets, Ed reached up and turned up the throttle to begin racing Betsy's engine. It started to roar with a mighty force like a huge jet engine. Betsy started to show signs of weakening a little, and Ed asked, "Betsy, are you all right girl?" Betsy's headlights still shone bright, but something was wrong. Betsy was getting weaker and weaker. Her pump pressure was getting lower and lower, and soon it was almost down to nothing. All of a sudden, a huge cloud of white smoke came out of Betsy's exhaust pipe. The fifty-year-old fire truck was showing no signs of life. Betsy's headlights became dim. Ed panicked and yelled for Chief Lou. "Help me! Help me! Betsy is sick. Something is very wrong."

Chief Lou came running, only to find that Betsy was leaking oil all over the place and that her engine had slowed down so much that finally—in front of all the firefighters, Chief Engineer Ed, and Chief Lou—Betsy took one big, deep breath and stopped working.

The firefighters lost their spirit. The secret of Berg was in trouble. They asked the fire chief, "What are we going to do?" Chief Lou ran to the phone to call the best mechanic in the land. The mechanic said to Chief Lou, "I can visit the fire station first thing in the morning to see if I can help." That night, twenty-five men and women pushed Old Betsy back into the firehouse. Chief Lou called a neighboring town to see if the town of Berg could borrow a spare fire engine until Betsy could be fixed and put back in service. Everyone who had been at the training that night had a heavy heart and wondered if Old Betsy could be saved.

The next day, the mechanic came with lots of tools and tried to start the old fire truck up, but Betsy wouldn't start. In fact, things just didn't look good at all. The mechanic looked into Betsy's headlights and said to her, "Well old girl, there's nothing I can do to make you better." Betsy smiled and said, "I think it's time for me to retire. My pump doesn't work, and my engine is worn out after fifty years. Tell Chief Lou I am sorry, but I can't go on any longer."

Chief Lou called a special meeting that night to tell then men and women of the fire department the bad news about Old Betsy. Chief Engineer Ed cried out, "It can't be true; Betsy's my best friend." Firefighter Rob said, "She saved my life at the old Simpson fire." Judy cried out, "It can't be true. She helped me save little John Jones, who got stuck in the manhole on Johnson Street." Everyone on the Berg Volunteer Fire Department became quiet for a moment while Chief Lou read the Firefighter's Prayer over the front engine of Old Betsy. After reading the prayer, Chief Lou started to cry and said to Old Betsy, "We love you, Betsy."

The department members cried as Betsy whispered to Chief Engineer Ed, saying, "You need to buy a new fire engine bigger and better than me so the new fire engine can protect the growing town of Berg.

Fire Chief Lou went to the mayor of the town and told him the bad news. The mayor called a special meeting of the town council to report the bad news about old Betsy. The head of the town council told Chief Lou to buy a new truck, but wondered what to do with Betsy. "Chief Lou," they said, "We don't have any room to keep Betsy in the fire station." "We will have to sell old Betsy to the scrapyard for salvage," said Chief Lou. The Mayor said, "We will keep that in mind until we get the new truck." "By the way, Chief, how soon can we get a new fire truck?" "I will have to check to see who may have one ready for immediate delivery," said Chief Lou. "The company that built Old Betsy went out of business a long time ago." The chief called all the fire truck companies in the country before he found one who had a new fire engine ready for delivery.

The fire truck company the chief found was the only one with a new fire engine available for sale. Chief Lou and Chief Engineer Ed visited the fire truck company. As they walked up to the doors of this huge factory, the company salesman greeted the two men.

He showed them the building where all the trucks where being built. Big new red trucks filled the entire building. Chief Lou asked the salesman, "Where's this new red fire engine?" The salesman stopped for a minute and said to the Chief, "Didn't they tell you about this fire truck? It's a little different from all these red trucks." The chief began to worry. He knew that the town of Berg needed a new fire truck like Old Betsy right now, but he had no idea what could be lying ahead. *Is this truck broken?* he wondered. *Are the tires flat? What can it be?* The salesman took the two men to the rear of the huge fire truck factory. It was dark, and there was a big cover over the only new fire truck available for the town of Berg.

The Chief said to the salesman, "Please uncover this truck so we can see what all the humbug is about!" As the salesman pulled back the cover, the problem began to appear. The new fire truck for the town of Berg wasn't a big and mighty red truck. This fire truck was painted

green. Chief Engineer Ed began to cry. He said, "How can this be; how can this green truck replace Old Betsy?" Fire Chief Lou remained silent. He looked the truck over from front to back. Then he walked to the front of the truck and looked into the headlights and whispered to the green fire truck, saying, "Are you ready to fill some big shoes?" Ed cried

out to the Chief, saying to him, "You can't be serious. A green fire truck? What will Betsy think about this little green fire truck replacing one of the bravest of all fire trucks?"

The little green fire truck smiled a little at Chief Lou and said, "If you will just give me a chance, you'll see I will make all of you proud." So Chief Lou and Chief Engineer Ed said to the salesman, "We will buy this little green fire truck." They drove the new fire truck home to the town of Berg. Before entering the town, Chief Lou called ahead to have all the town council and the firefighters stand by at the firehouse for the arrival of the brand-new fire truck. As Chief Lou and Chief Engineer Ed came to the edge of town, Chief Lou turned on

the red lights, blew the siren, and rang the bright silver bell to announce their arrival. As they came closer to the fire station, the crowd began cheering loudly for a brand new fire truck. The firefighters waited excitedly for new fire truck to arrive at the fire station. The air grew silent and a hush came over the crowd when the new green fire truck pulled up in front of the firehouse. A small voice came from the back of the crowd of townspeople and firefighters. "Oh no. How's that green truck gonna protect us?! It's ugly!"

Chief Lou climbed out on the new fire engine, smiled, and said to his firefighters, "This truck will make old Betsy proud. He can pump more water and carry more equipment, and most important of all, this truck has more character than any other fire truck in the world next to old Betsy." The mayor said, "Have you lost your mind? What are you saying?" Chief Lou said, "It's easy. Old Betsy earned our love by being ready 24 hours a day, 365 days a year. No matter what the time of day or weather outside, she was always ready to help anyone in need. Out of all the fire trucks being built at the fire truck company, only this little green truck told me he could live up to the work that Old Betsy had done over the years."

With that the crowd noticed that the headlights on the little green fire truck were growing brighter and brighter. Its mighty engine roared like a huge jet liner.

That was when the firefighters knew that the little green fire truck would help save the day. They unloaded the equipment from Old Betsy and the borrowed fire truck and began to put it all in the little green fire truck.

As the firefighters passed Old Betsy sitting on the driveway in front of the fire station, they noticed tears coming from Old Betsy's headlights. The new little green fire truck asked Betsy, "What's the matter?" Betsy said, "Since you're here now, I guess my next trip will be to the scrapyard." The little green fire truck said to Old Betsy, "Don't cry. Tell me about your town and how I should help the people in this town."

Betsy talked about all the fires she had gone to and how she had pumped through the night at the big lumberyard fire. She told the new little green fire truck about all the parades and how on special days the firefighters would take her to the park for all the children to play on. She said to the new truck, "Those were some of my best days, watching children turn my big steering wheel, ring my dull silver bell, and blow my siren. Those were the best of times." The green fire truck said to Betsy, "I hope I can live up to expectations." Then, as Betsy began to cry, the little green fire truck asked Betsy, "Where is the park?" Betsy shined her dull headlights forward and said, "Right there, across the street from the firehouse."

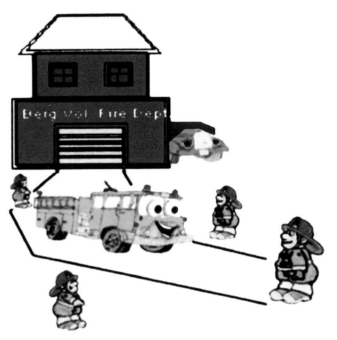

The little green fire truck was put into service right away, and Old Betsy was parked alongside the firehouse. A big blue tarp covered the front of Betsy. As the little green fire truck began to make runs every day, it became sad. The little green fire truck couldn't bear to see Old Betsy whither away to nothing while just waiting for the big old scrap wrecker to come and get her.

At the next drill night at the firehouse, an idea occurred to the little green fire truck. *I'll talk to Chief Engineer Ed about my idea.* He thought. *He will go for it and it will save Old Betsy.* The little green fire truck couldn't wait to see Ed. That night, Ed walked in the door, climbed into the little green fire truck, and said, "Come on, buddy; let's get this show on the road." That's when the little green fire truck said to Ed, "You have to listen to me. We have to save old Betsy!" "But how?" said Ed. The little green fire truck said, "What did Betsy like to do best?" "Well, she always liked to spend days in the park with all the children. She loved it when all the children climbed up in the seats, rang the bell, and blew her siren." The little green fire truck replied to Ed, "Why don't we park her in the park, facing our firehouse, so all the children can play on her all the time and she can watch over us?" Ed said to the little green fire truck, "That's a wonderful idea. I'll talk to Chief Lou about it. I am sure the mayor and the town council will like this idea as well."

So the next day, Chief Lou spoke to the mayor and the town council about placing Old Betsy in the park as a retirement spot. The Mayor and council agreed, so they prepared a space to park Old Betsy in the park right across the street from the firehouse.

At the next drill, the Mayor called for a special town celebration and retirement party for Old Betsy. All the people in town came to the park. Music was playing, and children were all aglow. Old Betsy was pulled into her final place for the entire community to see every day. As the firefighters helped slowly push Old Betsy into her spot, her headlights grew bright and the grill on the front of her engine began smiling. Old Betsy was still serving

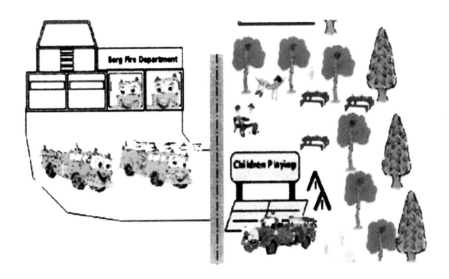

even though she was in retirement. She was there, where all the children she loved could play on her and imagine that someday they could be firefighters.

The moonlight shone down on Old Betsy and reflected across the street onto the fire station. That's where Buddy, the new green fire truck, stood on duty, ready to respond to any fire call.

Today the Berg Volunteer Fire Department has a new fire station with more space, and the town of Berg has grown up to be a city. The new fire station now has three green fire trucks

ready to serve the community. Just like Old Betsy, Chief Lou and Chief Engineer Ed retired from the fire department. The new chief, knowing the history of the Berg Volunteer Fire Department, knows that the landmark Old Betsy is still in the park, watching over the new fire trucks, which all are painted green. The new fire chief, Tom, says to all the firefighters, "The first little green truck brought to our community gave us pride when Old Betsy couldn't any longer. It's not easy being the only little green fire truck, but now with brothers and sisters sharing the same firehouse, the little green fire truck stands ready to protect and serve at all times while Old Betsy watches on!"

CPSIA information can be obtained
at www.ICGtesting.com
Printed in the USA
LVIC081122261212

313242LV00004B